Boise State University Western Writers Series   Number 27

George Catlin

By Joseph R. Millichap

Tulsa University

Editors: Wayne Chatterton
James H. Maguire

Business Manager:
James Hadden

Cover Illustration by George Catlin,
Courtesy of the Thomas Gilcrease
Institute of American History and
Art, Tulsa, Oklahoma. Cover Design
by Arny Skov, Copyright 1977.

Boise State University, Boise, Idaho

Library of Congress Card No. 77-76200

International Standard Book No. 0-88430-051-X

Printed in the United States of America by
The Caxton Printers, Ltd.
Caldwell, Idaho

George Catlin

George Catlin

George Catlin, the first and best observer of the Plains Indians, died in 1872, impoverished and ignored. As America enters its third century as a nation, it seems that American history might have caught up with him. In the 1970's Catlin at last is receiving the attention which is his due as an adventurer, as an anthropologist, and as an artist, both literary and graphic. His drawings, paintings, and lithographs are being shown in museums and libraries across the country; his most important book, *Letters and Notes on the Manners, Customs and Conditions of the North American Indians* (1841) has been republished in a very fine paperbound edition by Dover Press; and selections from *North American Indians* along with beautiful color reproductions have been edited for a new deluxe art volume. These publications will make easily accessible the accurate observation of the Plains Indian which has heretofore been the almost exclusive domain of those ethnologists who have had to dig up books long out of print. Several articles reappraising the life and works of Catlin have appeared in both popular and scholarly journals. Several more are planned, including a scholarly biography.

Like those well known Western observers Remington and Russell, Catlin is ultimately more important as a painter than as a writer. However, unlike his fellow artists, Catlin's writing is very specifically coordinated with his graphics. Therefore, the reader should consult some reproductions of Catlin's graphic art to complement his writing. Catlin is best read in well-illustrated volumes such as the Dover edition of *North American Indians,* Mooney's selected edition of that work, or Ross's edition of *Life Among the Indians* and his *Last Rambles.* These illustrations are black and white for the most part, but anyone can find good color reproductions in McCracken's *George Catlin and the Old Frontier;* Hunt and Rossi's *The Art of the West;* Brandon and Josephy's *The American Heritage Book of the American Indian,* and the new Time-Life Western Series volume on the Indians. Many good illustrated books about the West or the Indians include a few color reproductions, as do most historical or critical books about American art.

In recent years the improved accessibility of Catlin's work in both prose and paint has promoted a reawakened interest in what he has done; yet that work has always existed, even if it has been tucked away in the musty storerooms of museums and the dusty back shelves of libraries. The increased concerns with the West, with its history and art, with the Indian, with the uniqueness of the American experience, have all generated some of this new interest and accessibility.

But Catlin's work is now achieving popularity because history has caught up with him. At last Americans are ready to see with his essentially difficult vision. The American culture, which more or less ignored Catlin for several decades before his death and for a century afterward, has changed so radically that it is now ready to absorb an artistic vision which contradicts some of its most hallowed images of itself. In the creation of new self-images during the next century of the American experience, Catlin's work in both the literary and the graphic arts will make a significant contribution.

George Catlin is becoming an important literary and graphic artist for contemporary America because his close observation of the native American interprets the American experience through a complicated primitivism and a difficult, complex symbolism. A consideration of the American traditions of writing and painting reveals Catlin as a figure who not only combines these two art forms, but who also bridges the nineteenth and the twentieth centuries. In two mediums Catlin creates not only a moving, elegiac picture of the native American but also a romantic model of nature's nobleman. This figure is both a *memento mori*, a reminder of our own mortality and fallibility as a nation, and an *exemplum*, an illustration and ideal, for all Americans in both his day and ours. Catlin refused to portray a stereotyped or sentimentalized Indian. Instead he worked to depict the archetypal significance of the American primitive for civilized Americans, then and now. He insisted that his fellow countrymen see his point, and to this idealistic purpose he devoted his life.

And what a life it was. George Catlin was well-prepared to fulfill his purpose as the first artist observer of the American Indian. He was born in 1796 at Wilkes-Barre, Pennsylvania. At the time of his birth this town was a gateway to the frontier, much as St. Louis was in the 1830's, when he launched his western trips. Wilkes-Barre and the surrounding Wyoming Valley are also important in the history of white-Indian relations in America. In July 1778, eighteen years before Catlin's birth, the famed Wyoming Massacre shocked the fledgling nation. As Catlin later observed, history calls white-Indian struggles "battles" if the white side triumphs, "massacres" if the Indians win. During the Revolutionary War most of the Iroquois Confederacy remained loyal to Britain, probably because far-sighted leaders such as the Mohawk Joseph Brant saw that the Indian had more to fear from the land-hungry colonists than from the fur-hungry British traders. The Wyoming Valley fight was simply a skirmish between the Americans and the British, both sides being supported by their Indian allies. The Delawares were on the American side, the Iroquois on the British. The Iroquois, always fearsome warriors, swept their antagonists from the field and harried the Valley outposts. Catlin's mother, then only

7

seven years old, was captured by the hostile Iroquois. Yet she was released unharmed, and she evidently harbored no ill feelings against her captors. In fact, she always impressed upon young George the decency of her treatment.

George's father, Putnam Catlin, came to the Wyoming Valley from Litchfield, Connecticut, after an eight-year stint in the Revolutionary Army. He was a lawyer and land owner, an educated, fair-minded, free-thinking man, who held the local Indians in the greatest respect and who often attempted to record their history and culture. A year after George's birth, the family again moved to the Susquehanna Valley across the York State border.

George first met an Indian when he was out hunting with his first rifle at the age of nine. Taking aim at a ten-point buck, he was startled when another shot dropped the splendid animal. Out of the bushes emerged a giant Iroquois warrior, intent on skinning his kill. The frightened boy sighted down at this possible enemy, but lowered his rifle when he recognized their common humanity. Hiding himself until the Indian left, George then ran to tell his father about this poacher. Putnam Catlin welcomed the visitor to his land and discovered that the Indian was looking for a kettle of gold, which his father, one of Brant's warriors, had buried during the retreat from the 1778 battle. The Indian never found the kettle, but he became the fast friend of young George and presented him with a steel-bladed trade tomahawk when he left the area.

Two ironic developments followed. George was marked physically for life when the tomahawk rebounded from a playful throw at a tree and split his cheek open. This scar became symbolic of the psychological mark which the manly bearing of his first Indian friend had made upon George. A few days later word reached the Catlins that the body of On-O-Gong-Way, the Iroquois friend, had been found. He had been shot twice in the back, evidently for the treasure which some Wyoming Valley resident believed the Indian had discovered.

George grew up as a frontier youth, hunting and fishing in the open country of the Susquehanna Valley, but also attending school at the Classical Academy in Wilkes-Barre. The Susquehanna country of Catlin's boyhood seems to have been much like the Mississippi Valley when Sam Clemens was a boy, and Catlin whiled away his youth, like Tom Sawyer, "with books reluctantly held in one hand, a rifle or fishing pole grasped firmly and affectionately in the other" (*Letters and Notes on the Manners, Customs, and Conditions of the North American Indians*, London, 1841, 2 vols. Hereafter this long title will be abbreviated to *NAI*).

His father intended him for the law, and accordingly in 1817 he was sent to the famous Gould and Reeve Law School in Litchfield, Connecticut. After passing the bar in 1819 he returned to practice for two years in Pennsylvania, as "a sort of *Nimrodical* lawyer" (*NAI*, I, 2).

Long an illustrator by avocation, Catlin often whiled away the time drawing judges, defendants, and lawyers at his trials. At twenty-four Catlin soon sold all his possessions "save rifle and fishing tackle" (*NAI*, I, 2) in order to equip himself as a miniaturist. He made a comfortable living painting miniature portraits, which were then all the rage, and later graduated to oils on canvas. His early subjects included Sam Houston, DeWitt Clinton, and Dolly Madison. A good example of his early studio work is his self-portrait, painted in 1824 when he was twenty-eight years old. Although the romantic conventions of the Byronic pose somewhat mask the subject's individuality, no one looking at the picture can doubt the sincerity, the idealism, and the strength of this young man.

Catlin's problem at this time was that no purpose worthy of his strengths had presented itself. He wanted to be much more than a fashionable portraitist. This career he felt was no life for a real artist. Instead it would be a graveyard for his talents, as indeed it was for many more talented American painters. The 1820's was a decade of emerging American nationalism in the arts. Bryant, Irving, and Cooper were creating the first great American literature; Cole, Durand, and others in the Hudson River School were creating the first distinctively American painting. It was an exhilarating time to be an American, in this decade just before the American renaissance fully flowered with the publication of Emerson's *Nature* in 1836. Catlin wanted to be in the forefront of this American explosion in the arts, but he could not accomplish this purpose in New York or Philadelphia.

His problem was solved in a shock of recognition that he experienced when he viewed a party of Western Indians who were traveling to Washington for treaty negotiations in 1823.

> Black and blue cloth and civilization are destined, not only to veil, but to obliterate the grace and beauty of Nature. Man, in the simplicity and loftiness of his nature, unrestrained and unfettered by the disguises of art, is surely the most beautiful model for the painter,— and the country from which he hails is unquestionably the best study or school of the arts in the world: such I am sure, from the models I have seen, is the wilderness of North America. And the history and customs of such a people, preserved by pictorial illustrations, are themes worthy the life-time of one man, and nothing short of the loss of my life, shall prevent me from visiting their country, and of becoming their historian. (*NAI*, I, 2)

Aside from the psychological importance of this experience to Catlin's biography, this passage presents the Romantic aesthetic prevalent in that decade. Nature is what makes art; therefore, a great natural subject matter will make a great art. In fact, artifice has no place in art. Nature "has a grace beyond the reach of art" which can be touched only by spontaneous enthusiasm.

Catlin certainly possessed the enthusiasm. He carefully planned his excursion to the wilderness, though he took the time to paint enough portraits to warrant his election to the National Academy in 1826. He read books about the West and about the Indian, and he practiced his art by visiting Eastern Indian reservations and enclaves, painting figures such as Red Jacket, chief of the Senecas. This painting, his first Indian portrait, elicited such adverse reaction from a public which had been schooled in stereotyped noble savages that Catlin momentarily doubted his purpose. In 1830 he traveled to St. Louis, which was at that time the gateway to the great West. Here he became the protegé of General William Clark (of Lewis and Clark fame), who was then Superintendent of Indian affairs for the entire West. Clark was genuinely interested in the welfare of the Indian, and he had already begun a collection of Indian art and of white men's art which featured Indians. He quickly recognized Catlin's talents, and Clark took the young painter with him on treaty-making excursions to Wisconsin and Kansas. In 1831 Catlin at last saw the Plains Indians in their native state on the Upper Platte, as he visited the villages of the Grand Pawnee, Oto, Kansa, and Missouri tribes. Many years later, Catlin said he travelled even farther up the Platte and across the Rockies in the summer of 1831. This claim seems rather doubtful, however, in terms of existing evidence.

In the summer of 1832 Catlin made his most important trip among the Indians. He accepted the invitation of Pierre Chouteau, the frontier entrepreneur, to ride the *Yellowstone,* the first steamboat to attempt a trip up the Missouri to Fort Union at the mouth of the Yellowstone River, in what is now eastern Montana. On the slow upriver voyage there was plenty of time to visit villages of the upper Missouri tribes, such as the various Sioux villages. He also visited the Poncas, the Assineboines, and the Riccarees, but among the various bands of the Sioux he recorded the most noble portraits, fascinating ceremonials such as a dog feast held in his honor, and exciting scenes of the chase.

At Fort Union he had similar experiences. Here he also met the Blackfoot and Crow tribes, who had come from the mountains for their yearly trading. He painted many striking portraits and observed more hunting scenes, such as the buffalo chases. After several weeks at the fort, Catlin decided to descend the river by canoe, so that he could meet and paint the Indians he had missed journeying upstream. He hired two trappers as boatmen and set off on his greatest and most productive adventure.

About two hundred miles down river from Fort Union, he stopped at the village of the Mandans. His experience among these proud people was unique in many ways, as unique as the mysterious Mandans themselves. The tribe, now almost extinct, was a branch of the great Siouan family who had made its way from the midwest into the Upper Missouri country almost a millennium earlier. They were agricultural people, as well as hunters and pottery makers, who built fortified villages of large earth-covered houses. The Mandans were also interesting in appearance. As Catlin tells us, many seemed almost white, with hazel, blue, and gray eyes complemented by every shade and color of hair, except auburn or red. The unknown origin of these blond Mandans had already provoked speculation that they were a lost Jewish or Welsh tribe that had somehow emigrated to the Upper Missouri. Catlin, of course, subscribed to this Romantic theory, and its lack of scientific support did not hinder his accurate observation of almost every phase of their culture.

Apparently these intelligent people were as interested in Catlin as he was in them. They made him welcome, posed happily for his portraiture, and feasted him with buffalo ribs and prairie turnips. In the Mandan village he was as much the social lion as he would be a decade later in London and Paris.

In particular, he became the special friend of two of the most powerful men in the tribe, Mah-To-He-Ha, the Old Bear, a medicine man, and the illustrious Mah-To-Toh-Pa, the four Bears, second War Chief of the tribe. The sketch on the cover of this pamphlet depicts Mah-To-Toh-Pa being painted by Catlin.

Mah-To-Toh-Pa is a fascinating figure. A great warrior, as evidenced by the symbolic buffalo horns which only the most notable of men might wear, he was also an intelligent leader, an artist, a philosopher, and a gentleman. In short, he perfectly supported the theory of nature's nobleman dwelling in the wilderness, a theory which Catlin so much wanted to believe. Catlin was made a present of the robe shown in the picture; Mah-To-Toh-Pa had painted the robe himself.

The chief also explained the meaning of the symbols to the white artist. The adventures represented in the picture are breathtaking in their daring, and Catlin devoted a whole letter in *North American Indians* to their narration. For example, the spear which Four Bears holds had once belonged to a Riccaree chief, who left it in the body of Four Bear's brother. Vowing revenge, the Mandan chief waited for four years without meeting his brother's slayer in combat. Eventually he could wait no more and made his way alone, armed only with the spear, into the Riccaree village some two hundred miles away from the Mandan village. Here he killed the enemy, escaping with spear and scalp, and made his way back, pursued by the entire Riccaree tribe. Another picture showed him attacking the Assinneboines, where he earned his name. Deserted by the Mandans and their allies the Minatarees, the chief rushed the enemy alone, who later said he charged like four grizzly bears.

Catlin's friendship with Mah-To-He-Ha, the Old Bear, a man of great medicine, proved even luckier for the artist. As shown in one of Catlin's most famous pictures, the Old Bear wears his ceremonial vestments of animal relics, particularly the otter skin, and sacred plants. The Mandans considered Catlin's realistic painting to be great medicine or mystery. In fact, Mah-To-He-Ha had Catlin taken into the medicine society, the Mandan Academy, as it were, so that he was privileged to witness the most sacred rites of the tribe. Fortunately for the artist and posterity, he was present at the time when the willow leaves were full grown under the bank of the river. This was the time for O-Kee-Pa, the sacred rite celebrating the deliverance of the Mandans from a deluge, which was signaled when a bird went forth from their big canoe and returned with a willow branch. This ceremony is detailed in several chapters of *North American Indians,* and Catlin's accounts have been of great importance to modern anthropologists. Even more important is the sympathetic depiction of these ceremonies by an artist skilled in both paint and prose.

Soon after the O-Kee-Pa ceremonies, Catlin left the Mandans, continuing down the Missouri to the Mississippi and then to St. Louis. He spent the year 1833 in the East, assembling his Indian pictures and showing some of them in Pittsburgh and Cincinnati. In 1834 he was back on the plains—this time, however, on the plains of the Southwest. Travelling up the Arkansas, he arrived at Fort Gibson, which was then the center of the newly established Indian Territory. Here Catlin visited the Five Civilized Tribes that had lately come over the Trail of Tears from the Eastern lands appropriated by President Jackson. He painted such notables as John Ross, of the Cherokees, Sam and Ben Perryman of the Creeks, and Peter Pinchlin of the Choctaws. The latter "very gentlemanly man," as Catlin calls him (*NAI,* II, 123), was named Ha-Tchoo-Tuck-Nee, the Snapping Turtle. He gave Catlin "much curious and valuable information, of the history and traditions of his tribe" (*NAI,* II, 123). Much like the modern Oklahoma Indian artist Jerome Tiger, Catlin was particularly fascinated by the Choctaw ball play. Catlin also did several studies of Choctaw dances and ceremonies.

But his real interest was in the wild tribes, not in the civilized ones. Therefore he was impatient to leave with the column of dragoons under General Leavenworth and Colonel Dodge, a company which was to demonstrate the might of the U.S. Army to the Southwestern "savages," particularly the Comanches. The expedition left Fort Gibson on June 19th, with the temperature at 108. This was an inauspicious start to a very difficult trip. They visited, or were visited by, the Osage, whom Catlin called the tallest race of men in North America, and the Comanches, whom Catlin considered the world's greatest horsemen. He saw the Pawnee Picts, the Kiowas, and the Wicos. The white soldiers were much more impressed by the fierce Comanches than the Indians were by the bedraggled column of dragoons, because Oklahoma heat and bad water had decimated the ranks with fever. Many died, and Catlin himself lay helpless in the Comanche village while the column visited the Pawnees. The artist was most interested in the Comanche's manner of capturing wild horses, a method to which he devoted several illustrations and a full chapter in *North American Indians*. Yet he was eager to return to the comparative comfort of Fort Gibson, where he spent several weeks recovering from his bout with the fever. After his recovery, taking only his faithful horse Charley and his rifle, he rode alone to St. Louis, where he rejoined his wife and travelled with her to Florida. There he fully recuperated during the next winter.

Over the next three years Catlin interspersed short trips to the Indian country with short presentations of his gallery to the public. In early 1835 he travelled to the Upper Mississippi, visiting the Ojibways (or Chippewas), woodland people who lived in birch bark lodges and who travelled as much by canoe and snowshoes as they did by horseback. Catlin also met the Eastern Sioux, who had fallen on hard times because white-encouraged bounty hunting had destroyed their game. The artist could not help moralizing upon the comparative conditions of the two major branches of this large tribe, and he concluded that the touch of civilization was death for the Indian.

Yet the very next summer (1835) Catlin engaged in rather negative behavior when he became the first white man to visit the great pipestone quarry near the St. Peters River, in the territory of the Eastern Sioux. The Indians tried to dissuade him from visiting this sacred area, but Catlin ignored their objections in order to satisfy his curiosity. His act was one of bravado, because he defied a large band of armed Sioux. Moreover his behavior was a direct violation of his earlier strictures on preserving the integrity of the Indian. The sacred red pipestone, found only at this place, is now called catlinite in honor of its white discoverer.

This puzzling contradiction in Catlin's attitude toward the Indian becomes more obvious in the second phase of his career. This phase began after he had returned from the Pipestone Quarry trip, although he painted a few other Indians over the next few years, such as Osceola, The Black Drink, who was the intrepid chief of the Florida Seminoles. In this portrait, Osceola is depicted in all of his manly splendor—much unlike his state when Catlin later saw him in 1838 at Fort Moultrie, South Carolina. There the chief sat sick and dying, yet still encumbered by the chains which symbolized his capture when the United States forces betrayed a flag of truce. This was an act, Catlin comments, that an Indian could never bring himself to do. Walt Whitman's poem, "Osceola," was based on Catlin's portrait, which hung in the living room of Whitman's Camden house. But Catlin's field painting was essentially over for almost the next two decades, for this was the period of his exhibitions.

In 1837 his Indian Gallery opened in New York City, which was then, as now, the center of the entertainment world. In all

16

respects—critical, financial, even moral—his gallery was a success. Catlin never forgot his real purpose even in the midst of a Barnum-like showmanship that was necessary for any entertainment venture at that time. His lectures were exciting, but also documentary, sensible, and very sympathetic to the Indian. He proposed, for example, that all the prairie areas from the Mississippi to the Rockies should be preserved as a vast Indian reservation, where the native American could live in his natural splendor. Opinions such as this were not calculated to win him much popularity in the expansionist America of the late 1830's. In fact, his championship of the Indian probably cost him his major opportunity for financial success—the attempted sale of his entire gallery to the United States Government, which was to form the basis of a national gallery of art and science. The sale fell through because Southerners were opposed to the idea of keeping the plains covered with Indians and buffaloes rather than slaves and cotton. Scenes like Catlin's, done in nature's wilderness, had little appeal for the American who was fascinated with an image of a paying garden, the plantation.

Yet for all this idealism Catlin very much expected and worked hard to achieve real financial reward for his Indian endeavors. He wanted to be a moral leader, but he also wanted to be well paid for the position. This paradoxical desire has existed in the American character since the Pilgrims came ashore at Plymouth. Perhaps this paradox in the American character is, at least partly, what is really meant by that ambiguous term —the American dream.

Catlin was a great American dreamer. When Congress balked at the purchase of his collection, he shipped it off to England, hoping to whip up American chauvinism by threatening to sell the whole lot to some more discerning foreign collector, perhaps to the hated British government itself. After all, he had a connection at court in the person of the Honorable C. A. Murray,

17

Master of Her Majesty's household, and an old acquaintance of Catlin's from the Upper Mississippi. On February 1, 1840, Catlin opened his famous exhibition at the Egyptian Hall in Piccadilly. In one section were arranged the portraits; in another were landscapes; in others were ceremonials, games, sports, amusements; and one section contained several sorts of Indian artifacts. His reception was grand. The Egyptian Hall was visited by noblemen and men of science. The British press was even more lavish in praise than were their American counterparts, and the public flocked through the doors at a shilling a head.

In 1841 Catlin published his first and best book, the *North American Indians*. It, too, was critically well received, though it was not a complete financial success. Catlin, now 45 years old, was at the zenith of his career. From 1841 on, his fortunes were on the decline.

The fickle London public soon tired of Indian pictures; so Catlin started putting on Indian shows, at first with painted cockneys wearing buckskins taken from his collection, and later with a group of Ojibway Indians, Canadian subjects of Her Majesty who were touring England at the time. The "Hobjibways," as the cockneys called them, revived some interest in Catlin's work. He even wangled an invitation to see the Queen. Later he secured the services of some real plains Indians, fourteen Iowas who had been brought to Europe by a well-meaning clergyman. Again the public returned to Catlin's gallery. Again Catlin published, this time his *North American Indian Portfolio of Hunting Scenes and Amusements,* including twenty-five lithographs.

This publishing venture proved to be a financial disaster. Evidently his Indian talent shows were an aesthetic disaster to accompany the monetary one. No less a critic than Charles Dickens wrote of the troupe as "wretched creatures . . . their dances no better than a chorus of Italian opera in England." In fact, many Englishmen objected to Catlin's exploitation of his Indian actors. In his favor it should be said that he did not bring the Indians over, that he treated them fairly, and that he helped to get them home again. Yet he did not hesitate to use them when his show was failing.

When the English audience tired of even the real Indians, Catlin and the Iowas trouped off to Paris, where they received a warm welcome. France was the home of Rousseau's noble savage. Again Catlin was lionized. He met authors, artists, and King Louis Phillipe, who had once floated the Mississippi during his period of exile. Again it seemed that fortune was favoring Catlin.

Then disasters started to accumulate. Three of the Iowas died of various white diseases. In 1845 Catlin's wife died of pneumonia. He procured the services of another Ojibway group, and several of them died of smallpox. He nursed the rest at his own expense. His attempts to sell the collection failed. He had to mortgage it, and ultimately lost it. His book on the European travels, *Catlin's Notes of Eight Years Travels and Residence in Europe* (1848), was a complete failure, financial and critical. Then, his little son, Georgie, died of typhoid. This was the final blow. Catlin, at 52, was a broken man.

The story of his healing, his resurrection, is a fascinating one, but one which must be abbreviated here because it has only a slight connection with the heart of Catlin's achievement and with the American West. Often the artist submerges beyond the biographer's sight. It is known that his Gallery was seized by his creditors; his daughters were taken away by his rich in-laws; and his pride was shattered by denunciations of his work by jealous rivals, in particular, by Henry Schoolcraft, the self-styled ethnologist who angled the congressional support which Catlin deserved. Down and out in London, Paris, and Brussels, Catlin suddenly reappeared on a ship to South America. Ostensibly on an expedition seeking gold, the artist was soon painting

19

the South American Indians: the Caribbees, Connibos, Auca, and many others. With a single companion, a giant Cuban named Cesar, he ascended the Amazon to its headwaters, crossed the Andes to Lima, took a ship up the Pacific coast to Alaska, and met the Indians of the Northwest—the Salish, the Flatheads, the Shoshones. He also saw the Southwestern Indians—the Mohaves, the Yumas, and the Apaches. Then he canoed down the Rio Grande to Matamores and returned to Europe. In 1856, he made a shorter South American tour. Soon new books were flowing from his pen, and new scenes were appearing at his easel. In 1857 he published *Life Among the Indians*, in 1867 *O-Kee-Pa*, in 1871 *Last Rambles Among the Indians*. In neither prose nor painting are these later works the equal of his earlier products. Yet he was working. At last, in 1870, at the age of 74, Catlin returned to the United States to stay. For his last two years he tried to sell his paintings to the Smithsonian. He was still unsuccessful. While he was staying with his daughters in Jersey City in 1872, he died.

Like so many figures in our early literature and art, especially in our Western literature and art, Catlin had to wait for an audience that had been educated by modern writers and painters before people could appreciate his matter, understand his forms, and comprehend his vision. Although Catlin's writing and painting unite the best impulses in the early Romantic movement, he was largely ignored by his contemporaries. An important exception is Charles Baudelaire. In his famous review of the Salon of 1846, Baudelaire unreservedly praises Catlin as a man and artist. He speaks of beauty and superb elegance, applauding the choice of subject matter and technique, but particularly the use of color. Portraits such as that of Stu-Mick-O-Sucks, The Buffalo Back Fat, from the 1846 Salon, or hunt scenes such as Buffalo Chase from the Salle Valentino Exhibition, represented for Baudelaire the primal energy which he also saw in Delacroix's and Fromentin's rendering of North African primitives.

The jaded arch-sophisticate sought in the primitive life a combination of Romantic art's two great matters—Nature and the Past. In Baudelaire's words, "In their fine attitudes and their ease of movement these [Catlin's] savages make antique sculpture comprehensible" (*The Mirror of Art,* p. 73) .

Catlin's aesthetic posits a similar connection of the primitive life and the classic past.

> I have for a long time been of opinion, that the wilderness of our country afforded models equal to those from which the Grecian sculptors transferred to the marble such inimitable grace and beauty; and I am now more confirmed in this opinion, since I have immersed myself in the midst of thousands and tens of thousands of these knights of the forest; whose whole lives are lives of chivalry, and whose daily feats, with their naked limbs, might vie with those of the Grecian youths in the beautiful rivalry of the Olympian games.
> (*NAI,* I, 15)

He continues to catalogue the "scenes of beauty and wildness which may be daily witnessed in that romantic country" (*NAI,* I, 15) , thus equating classic beauty and the natural vitality of primal cultures. Mah-To-Toh-Pa, the Four Bears, Second Chief of the Mandans, confirms Catlin's notion of the classic and the natural as one. Stoic, dignified, calm, the Indian leader assumes the pose of a classical orator. It is almost as if George Washington, in one of his classical metamorphoses on canvas, had donned the buckskin, fur, and feathers of the Indian.

The same classic dignity with its traditional head-and-shoulders shots rather than full-length poses appears in the portraits from the 1845 Salon which so impressed Baudelaire. In either form, and among all varieties of Indians, Northwest and Southwest, Woodland and Plains, wild and semi-civilized, Catlin's portraiture retains the same effects. He knew first-hand the natural virtues which his subjects possessed, and he developed the uncanny facility to capture with a few quick strokes the essence of both strong individuality and the collective strength which the Native American drew from his heritage.

Catlin's portraits rank with any American Romantic work in that form, and his Indians in both graphic and written depiction perhaps outdo any white renditions in the Nineteenth Century. The sentimentalized "noble red men" of painters, such as Rindisbacher or West, as well as of poets like Freneau, Bryant, and a dozen lesser ones, deserve no more serious comparison to Catlin's portraits than do the howling savages of Puritan sermons, of captivity narratives, of Franklin's *Autobiography,* and of Vanderlyn's "The Death of Jane McCrea." Cooper's Chingachgook pales by comparison with Catlin's two chapters on Mah-To-Toh-Pa, while Cooper's Magua is a dusky stereotype drawn from white sexual hysteria. Longfellow does not create any figure much better than Chingachgook, even though Longfellow read Catlin and drew upon his descriptions for scenes in *Hiawatha.* Melville's Indians are real characters, not symbolic bundles of civilized virtues or vices, but they are few and briefly developed in comparison with Catlin's myriad North American Indians.

In the graphic arts, Eastman seems stiff by comparison, Bodmer too clinical, Miller too Romantic. The Indians of these painters seem kidnapped from textbooks, calendars, or light opera. Not until Remington and Curtis begin to realistically paint and photograph Indians toward the end of the century did Catlin have any real competition for artistic honors, and their works lack the romance of Catlin's vision. Catlin presents the most natural and the most artistically compelling Indians in American literature or painting.

The Romantic attitude toward nature, formed and ordered by the Romantic attitude toward the past, pervades all of Catlin's works, literary and graphic. In his painting, this combination

22

of artistic themes is most evident in his landscapes. They demonstrate that Catlin was not a great landscape painter, but they present an attitude toward nature common to the landscape artists of the period, particularly those of the Hudson River School.

Catlin was associated with Thomas Cole at Peale's Academy in the early 1820's. By 1832 Catlin's vision had become fixed upon the figure of the Indian in the landscape, but he was also working out the same Romantic impulses which find expression in the more refined canvases of Cole, Durand, Church, and others of the period. Yet for all of Catlin's limitations as a landscapist, he has a vigor which is somewhat vitiated in more academic works such as Cole's "The Ox-Bow," which is unified by the painter's easel on the hillside, or Durand's "Kindred Spirits," which is intellectualized by the figures of Bryant and Cole rather stuffily contemplating the Catskill cove.

In his view of the Missouri, the natural flow of the river and hills, though crudely presented, seems more naturally unified by the figure of the solitary Indian, overlooking his grassy domain. Catlin also describes and depicts this plastic nature as "some ancient city in ruins" (*NAI*, I, 19), reiterating the theme of the past. Here the country is so raw that the artist must invent an imaginary past so that it may be comprehensible. The allegorical landscapes of Cole and minor American Romantic painters, which combine the American countryside with a heavy influence of the classical past, are clearly analogous to Catlin's effect in this combination of painting and poetic prose. The theme is also prominent in literature—in Bryant's "The Prairies," for instance, where he erroneously attributes the Indian mounds to a lost race. Irving, in *A Tour on the Prairies,* and Cooper, in *The Prairie,* also work to invest the open new country with the traditional values of the picturesque and the sublime, drawn from the scenery of the Lake Country and the Catskills. For the Romantics the picturesque involved subjects and scenes which were quaint, interesting, and colorful; the sublime involved those visions which were truly beautiful and elevating. Catlin was also aware of the true sublimity of his scene. He was aware of its vast size and scope. His monochromatic hills and lucid skies symbolically capture the heartland of America more effectively than does the work of any other artist of the Nineteenth Century.

In the equivalent of the Romantic genre painting of the era—scenes of animals, hunting, and the movements and occupations of the Indians—Catlin is a much finer artist. In these scenes, landscape is only secondary and even more stylized, yet this stylization creates an even greater sense of the simple power inherent in nature, in the earth itself. The hills in his buffalo hunts are like the breasts of the Nature goddess-mother, the feminine complement to the masculine principle, the spears and arrows and rampaging horses of the hunters. The universal grass nourishes the buffalo, who in turn provide sustenance for primitive man. In these scenes Catlin reaches his greatest energy, not simply because of the excitement of the chase, but even more because here he symbolically realizes the complementary worlds of male and female, man and nature, past and present. The archetypal significance of the hunt which animates so much great American literature, from Melville's *Moby Dick* to Faulkner's *Go Down, Moses,* also finds vital expression in Catlin's painting and prose.

Even the animals bristle with this archetypal energy. Surely a hunter would be as loath to face such a lowering Buffalo Bull as the whaler would be to face the average sperm whale. Who ever saw buffalo like these? They are as big as railroad locomotives, black as night. In motion they are as fleet as deer. They come charging out of some paleolithic nightmare onto Catlin's canvases. His bears are just as fearsome, bigger than two or three men, likewise black as night, covering forty feet a jump. They are ancestors of Faulkner's Old Ben, just as Sam Fathers is a distant relative of Catlin's stoic chiefs.

A painting of a ceremonial, such as the "Sioux Bear Dance," demonstrates Catlin's concern with the evocation of a primitive unity of man with nature similar to that of the hunt scenes themselves. His late version, dated 1847, amplifies an earlier, smaller canvas which concentrates on the ring of dancers. Aside from the inherent qualities of the subject itself, Catlin's composition, style, and colors also project his theme. Compared to his field sketch and his first version, the central group of figures is more tightly and compactly organized, with greater duplication and stylization in their poses. In particular, their hands, deliberately held so as to imitate the grizzly's forepaws when standing on his hind legs, are exaggerated and emphasized by Catlin's composition and by the trick of placing bear claws on the costumed dancer's arms. The complementary motif of animal fur is picked up in their ankle decorations and the crossing of their eagle plumes, which is in turn extended to the crosshatching of the teepees, onward into the distant trees, and at last off into the horizon. Everything in the composition of the painting expands the central grouping into the natural world, which is mystically ordered and encompassed by the perfect circle of the dance itself.

The more complex the ceremony, the more complex Catlin's description and depiction of it become. A good example is his portrayal of the Buffalo Bull Dance of the Mandan. The Bear Dance previously described was a sort of impromptu affair preceding a hunt. But the Buffalo Bull ceremony is a part of the Mandan O-Kee-Pa, the holy season, during which the tribe celebrated its creation and its redemption from a deluge, worshipped the good spirit of the natural world which supported them, and initiated the young men into their mature responsibility in a terrifying torture rite. The forms of the ceremonies were minutely prescribed, so that Catlin's picture stresses the order of the quaternity symbols—the four groups of two buffalo dancers each, the four figures facing the four directions, the four drummers in the center near the medicine ark (sixteen figures—four fours altogether), and, above all, the four ceremonial staffs with their symbolic burdens. In the lower left hand corner, O-Kee-Hee-De, the evil spirit, is entering to disrupt this order. In a long, detailed, and thoroughly fascinating account, which takes up almost fifty pages of *North American Indians*, Catlin describes how O-Kee-Hee-De is ultimately thwarted and sent back into the wild prairie beyond the orderly square of the dance ground.

Catlin's prose description of O-Kee-Hee-De complements the drawings he later published.

> This strange character darted about in a zig-zag course in all directions on the prairie, like a boy in pursuit of a butterfly, until he approached the piquets of the village, when it was discovered that his body was entirely naked, and painted as black as a negro, with pounded charcoal and bear's grease; his body was therefore everywhere a shining black, except occasionally white rings of an inch or more in diameter, which were marked here and there all over him; and frightful indentures of white around his mouth, resembling canine teeth. Added to his hideous appearance, he gave the most frightful shrieks and screams as he dashed through the village and entered the terrified group. (*NAI*, I, 167)

The author's prose imagery underlines O-Kee-Hee-De's purpose in the ceremonials. The devil figure is an incarnation of animal passion which seems childish when uncontrolled in human character. Therefore his "shrieks and screams" issue through "canine" teeth as he darts across the prairie "like a boy in pursuit of a butterfly." Of course, he is really in pursuit of the village females, and he terrifies them with a phallic "wand or staff," suspended between his legs, "some eight or nine feet in length with a red ball on the end of it" (*NAI*, I, 167). But his formidable weapon is rendered useless by the power of the symbolic medicine pipe, and O-Kee-Hee-De is reduced to a figure of ridicule and chased from the village by the indignant women.

Catlin's portraits, analyzed earlier for their classical motifs, are also organized around the theme of nature. For example, the classic pose of Mah-To-Toh-Pa also demonstrates his situation as a literal nobleman of nature. The portrait is balanced between the line of the body and that of the spear, creating a flowing tension which Catlin often employs in scenes from nature. The pointed motif of spear-blade and its feathers also plays against the buffalo points and feathers of the headdress. All of these details, of course, symbolically represent the natural qualities of the man. The buffalo horn headdress is a mark of signal honor, worn only by the greatest hunters and heroes. During Catlin's visit only Mah-To-Toh-Pa, among all the Mandans, was allowed this privilege. The robe itself Catlin lengthens from an actual shirt (which was given to him by Four Bears and which is now at the Smithsonian) in order to gain room for detailing, as well as for gaining the effect of a classical toga. One of the major changes he effects is in the rosette or crest which adorns the robe, balancing the figure's head, and drawing attention down from the upward extension lines. The crest represents the sun, and Catlin's colorful exaggeration of it clearly dramatizes the masculine role of the great chief, his role as the life-providing principle for his famly and his tribe.

The famous dual portrait of Wi-Jun-Jon, the Pigeon's Egg Head, plays upon similar effects. Catlin had painted this Assineboin sub-chief on his way to Washington in 1831. Later, he composed this full-figure as a comparison to support his earlier observations about the classic dignity inherent in the natural life. His prose description from *North American Indians* effectively complements the pictures.

> He was dressed in his native costume, which was classic and exceedingly beautiful . . . ; his leggings and shirt were of the mountain-goat skin, richly garnished with quills of the porcupine, and fringed with locks of scalps, taken from his enemies' heads. Over these floated his long hair in plaits, that fell nearly to the ground; his head was decked with the war-eagle's plumes—his robe was of the skin of the young buffalo bull, richly garnished and emblazoned with the battles of his life; his quiver and bow were slung, and his shield, of the skin of the bull's neck.
>
> He had in Washington exchanged his beautifully garnished and classic costume, for a full dress "en militaire." . . . It was, perhaps, presented to him by the President. It was broadcloth, of the finest blue, trimmed with lace of gold; on his shoulders were mounted two immense epaulettes; his neck was strangled with a shining black stock, and his feet were pinioned in a pair of waterproof boots, with high heels, which made him "step like a yoked hog." (*NAI,* II, 196)

Catlin's verbs perfectly capture in language the visual effect in the lines of the "after" picture—the awkward angle of the figure, the confused lines created by the bottles, umbrella, and sword, the supercilious molding of the facial features around the stubby cigarette which has replaced the beautiful calumet of the "before" shot. The noble savage has degenerated into a figure like the swaggering bandit chief from some Western movie.

Wi-Jun-Jon's transformation also reiterates the theme of the past by foreseeing the future degeneration and destruction of the Indian before the juggernaut of advancing civilization. Catlin constantly plays on this elegiac theme, common to both serious and popular literature and graphics in his day. Unlike most of his fellow Americans, both artists and audience, Catlin really intended to convey the seriousness of this theme. He mourned the passing of the last great wilderness and of the primitive men who peopled it. Again and again he proposed a national park embracing the high plains and the Rockies, where the Indian might live in his primal splendor. Realistic enough to know that this dream would never come true, he did what he could to record the passing spectacle of Native American life. In both dream and reality he was also selfish, for he likewise wanted to escape into that primitive world.

Catlin seems closest to Thoreau among our early writers. The love of nature, the desire for the primitive state, the abomination of commerce and money, the accurate observation of nature, the anecdotes, the verbal wit are all characteristic of both writers. Catlin, of course, cannot approach Thoreau's genius in prose, but Thoreau does not draw as well as Catlin. Perhaps even more than the Concord natural philosopher, somewhat justifiably called parochial by Henry James, George Catlin in his very life symbolizes the soul of the American Romantic movement—the complementary desires for the primal past and the vitality of nature unchecked. In really living the "primitive and frontier life" which Thoreau called for, Catlin discovered savages as noble as Chingachgook—savages that were true American Adams in a Western Eden bridging the gulf of time to the primal man that was proclaimed by Walt Whitman. In all his talents—for adventure, for writing, and for painting—Catlin unifies the best of American Romanticism.

Even a brief analysis of Catlin's prose works will confirm the accuracy of such laudatory judgments, though the reader should keep in mind that prose was always a secondary medium for Catlin. He wrote his books around his pictures, and this method of composition accounts for the strengths and weaknesses of his writing. Therefore, Catlin reads best in well illustrated editions. Catlin's prose does more than merely to describe his pictures, however, and books such as the sparsely illustrated *Eight Years Travels* are interesting in their own right.

Although Catlin is ultimately more important as a painter, he is nevertheless a talented writer whose prose works should be much better known. Catlin was well educated in the classical tradition at Wilkes-Barre Academy, and in the law at Gould and Reeve's school. At his first school Catlin learned a fluent prose style which was strengthened by the logical rigor of his legal training. Catlin's work bristles with quotations from the classics, particularly from Virgil, and from the English writers, particularly from Shakespeare and Pope. His classical training provided him not only with a sense of the past and of the basic questions concerning the human condition, but also with a knowledge of literary art which he employed in his works. Occasionally he tends toward over-elaboration, both in the ornate redundance of the Eighteenth Century, as seen in Cooper, and in the overdone sublimity of the early Nineteenth Century, as seen in Emerson. However, Catlin's prose is generally straightforward and vigorous, remininiscent of Thoreau.

Form as well as style reminds his reader of the great Romantic artists in prose. He deals with the same matters—the Romantic themes of Nature and the Past—in forms as organically natural as Thoreau's cycle of the seasons at Walden or Melville's journeys out across the trackless oceans. Almost invariably Catlin uses the journey motif as his principle of organization. In *North American Indians* he carries his civilized prejudices to the wilds of the West. In *Eight Years Travel* he brings the Indians to the civilization of Europe. A further refinement occurs in the actual manner of his trips. Almost invariably he uses civilization's means, particularly the same steamboat which Twain symbolically utilizes in *Huck Finn*. But Catlin uses it to reach his desired end, the heart of the wilderness. He takes his steamboats up the Missouri, the Arkansas, the Amazon. Then he floats back by canoe or dugout, or rides out on horse or burro, or simply walks back to civilization. If a deep structure exists in Catlin's work, this is it—the immersion in the wilderness which he can leave only reluctantly, only by the most natural means of transportation. Clearly then, the structures of his books match their subjects—Catlin's impressions of the American Indian as a symbol of the primitive life, a primitive life which the civilized American can relinquish only with the utmost regret.

Like the first works of many American writers, Catlin's first book is his best and his most important work. It is also the book most relevant to the study of the American West, and therefore it should receive the most attention.

North American Indians began as a series of letters which Catlin wrote to the *New York Commercial Advertiser* during his Western trips. Evidently they were all written while he was in the wilderness and were sent directly to the newspaper. In 1839, when Catlin started to put the book together, he expanded these letters and composed others about events he had discussed or scenes he had not described earlier. For the most part, the author succeeds in maintaining the mood of excitement which marks his initial discovery of the Plains Indian in his native state. At only a few places in Volume II, where he catalogues a great number of miscellaneous portraits, does his book drag at all. In fact, the epistolary framework provides a stylistic distancing of the author from his material, a distancing which he does not achieve in his later books. In style as well as subject *North American Indians* is Catlin's most interesting book, and Volume I, the narrative of his 1832 Upper Missouri trip, is his single best work in terms of writing and theme, as well as of subject matter.

Since Catlin had actually written his first letter to the *Commercial Advertiser* from Fort Union at the mouth of the Yellowstone on June 17, 1832, he begins at this point. His first letter in *North American Indians* is an autobiographical preface which he coyly admits he had not written in 1832. This study draws upon this chapter in the biographical sketch above, but the chapter contains other interesting material. In particular, it contains a general discussion of his essential subject, the North American Indian. He makes two major points: that the Indians are "human beings, with features, thoughts, reasons, and sympathies like our own" (*NAI*, I, 5); and that their "term of existence has nearly expired" (*NAI*, I, 5). He develops a salient idea by insisting upon the essentially religious nature of the Native American culture. In turn, he points out that America was destroying its Indians because the young Republic lacked a religious sense.

> Their country was entered by white men, but a few hundred years since; and thirty millions of these are now scuffling for the goods and luxuries of life, over the bones and ashes of twelve millions of red men; six millions of whom have fallen victims to the small-pox, and the remainder to the sword, the bayonet, and whiskey; all of which means of their death and destruction have been introduced and visited upon them by acquisitive white men; and by white men, also, whose forefathers were welcomed and embraced in the land where the poor Indian met and fed them with "ears of corn and with pemican." Of the two millions remaining alive at this time, about 1,400,000 are already the miserable living victims and dupes of white man's cupidity, degraded, discouraged and lost in the bewildering maze that is produced by the use of whiskey and its concomitant vices; and the remaining number are yet unroused and unenticed from their wild haunts or their primitive modes, by the dread or love of white man and his allurements. (*NAI*, I, 6)

These are the subjects to which Catlin returns again and again. The largest part of his narrative attempts an accurate and sympathetic account of the Indian in his natural state, an account which Catlin confidently assumes will demonstrate the common humanity of white and red men. He spends a disproportionate amount of time in the discussion of the Indian's religious beliefs, customs, and ceremonies. His accounts are also punctuated by elegies concerning a race which he feels will not withstand the corrupt and corrupting touch of America's putative civilization. In description, narration, and argument, the book constantly projects the Romantic concern with Nature and the Past by showing the primal man in the state of nature and by comparing him with the civilized man in the confinements of society, a society which was rapidly engulfing the primitive life.

His first narrative chapter iterates these Romantic themes, as he describes "a voyage so full of incident, so many scenes of the picturesque and the sublime" (*NAI*, I, 14). His description of this "romantic" country proceeds in the same manner. For example, he writes of "hundreds of graceful youths, without a care to wrinkle, or a fear to disturb the full expression of pleasure and enjoyment that beams upon their faces—their long black hair mingling with their horses' tails floating in the wind, while they are floating over the carpeted prairie" (*NAI*, I, 15). These graceful figures are picturesque in the Romantic sense, but, more importantly, they lead Catlin toward the sublime vision of Nature.

Catlin is caught up in the very ecstasy of the primitive life when he has a chance to participate in a buffalo hunt.

> I have always counted myself a prudent man, yet I have often *waked* (as it were) out of the delirium of the chase (into which I had fallen, as into an agitated sleep, and through which I had passed as through a delightful dream), where to have died would have

been but to have remained, riding on, without a struggle or a pang. (*NAI*, I, 252)

This particular hunting party was organized by Kenneth McKenzie, the agent of Fort Union, in order to replenish a nearly empty larder, and the visiting Crows and Blackfeet soon joined in the chase. Catlin shot his buffalo, but he also ran his horse by the side of the Indians as they attacked their game with arrows and spears. In this manner he soon had material for his genre painting.

The process of picture-painting was a mystery of the highest order for the Indians assembled at the Fort, and after they had observed him artistically re-creating the buffalo and the rolling hills, he succeeded in persuading Stu-Mick-O-Sucks, the Buffalo's Back Fat, Chief of the Blackfeet, to sit for his portrait. After this dignitary was captured on a canvas which Baudelaire would praise thirteen years later in Paris, Catlin had begun his career as a portrait painter.

Although he was unaware of the fact at the time, he was very nearly out of business also. About a month earlier, when the *Yellowstone* had stopped at Fort Pierre, eight hundred miles below Fort Union, the agent had cajoled several visiting Sioux dignitaries to sit for Catlin. Among them was Mah-To-Chee-Ga, The Little Bear, Chief of the Onc-Pa-Pa Band. Catlin decided to do this handsome fellow in profile, and the artist had almost finished his portrait when the next sitter interrupted the proceedings. This Indian was Shon-Ka, The Dog, Chief of the Bad Points Band. He was known as a fearsome warrior of very ill disposition, and he lived up to his reputation by calling Little Bear "a half man." When challenged he pointed to Catlin's painting as corroboration for his insult. The white medicine artist had seen fit to paint only half of his subject's face. Little Bear replied that Shon-Ka was "a half woman," and a feud was on. Both men repaired to their teepees outside the walls of the Fort and returned with weapons. Little Bear did not realize that his wife, who did not know the circumstances of his anger, had removed the bullet from his flintlock so that he would not hurt anyone while in camp. When the antagonists saw each other they fired simultaneously. Shon-Ka escaped unscathed, but Little Bear fell dead with half of his face shot away—the half which Catlin had left out of the portrait. In a few minutes the Onc-Pa-Pa band was in pursuit of Shon-Ka and his band, a chase which lasted for several months and took the lives of several distinguished warriors.

The Indians also blamed Catlin for the bloodshed, and Pierre Chouteau hustled the artist onto the *Yellowstone,* which soon set out for Fort Union. Although Catlin was unaware of the circumstance, Little Bear's band also declared his life forfeit, along with Shon-Ka's. However, by the time they had tracked and killed the elusive chief of the Bad Points Band, Catlin had floated back past Fort Pierre and was on his way to the safety of St. Louis.

At Fort Union, a similar feud, which did not involve Catlin, provided the artist with his first chance to see a medicine man performing his mysteries. A Blackfoot warrior lay dying after being shot from ambush by a Knisteneaux chief, and the medicine man was called in. Catlin compares these mysteries to the last rites of a Christian church. He was even more fascinated by the Blackfoot doctor's unique vestments.

> Besides the skin of the yellow bear (which being almost an anomaly in that country, is out of the regular order of nature, and, of course, great medicine, and converted to a medicine use) , there are attached to it the skins of many animals, which are also anomalies or deformities, which render them, in their estimation, *medicine*; and there are also the skins of snakes, and frogs, and bats,—beaks and toes and tails of birds,— hoofs of deer, goats, and antelopes. . . . (*NAI,* I, 40)

In this same letter Catlin also discusses the whole subject of Indian mysteries, including the "medicine bag" and the entire idea of totemism. His succinct account neatly summarizes a very complex subject, and once again the account demonstrates not only Catlin's sympathy with the Indian but also his clear insight into the primitive strength of the Native American. The Indian, because of his religious unity with his world, becomes the perfect symbol of man in harmony with Nature and the Past. This is the wholeness so assiduously sought by the Romantics, both European and American.

Catlin's letters from Fort Union narrate his experiences, list the subjects of his painting, and, most importantly, illuminate various facets of Indian life. Letter No. 4 concerns the buffalo hunt; No. 5 describes Indian dress and accessories; No. 6, Indian religion; No. 7, Indian housing; No. 8, Indian hairstyles and cosmetic arts; No. 9, Indian personality or character. His formal discussions usually stem from some particular incident or illustration; but taken as a whole, these first nine chapters give a well-rounded description of Plains Indian life. Many of the details—scalps, peace pipes, medicine bags—are picturesque. Many of the personalities are striking. Many of the incidents are fascinating. For example, Catlin devotes several pages to the return of Wi-Jun-Jon and to the revulsion that his family and friends showed at his grotesque appearance. They stood for several moments in silence with their hands over their open mouths, an Indian sign for astonishment. Only after considerable time did any words pass between the prodigal and his people, and then their conversation was cold and formal. At last Wi-Jun-Jon had the chance to tell of the wonders he had witnessed in Washington. But almost to a man, his friends refused to believe him. He had stayed too long with the fork-tongued whites, they said; he had become a liar too. Eventually, when he persisted in his stories and his civilized airs, Wi-Jun-Jon was killed by the tribe because of his useless lies. Thus ended the sad story of the flight of Pigeon's Egg Head to civilization.

From Fort Union, Catlin descended the Missouri by canoe, in the company of two trappers, stopping to visit the tribes he had missed on the way upstream. The most important was his visit to the Mandan's permanent village near what is today Bismarck, North Dakota. On the way to the Mandan village Catlin records several adventures in which they hunt buffaloes and are in turn hunted by bears. He also indulged in a dialogue with Baptiste, one of the guides, about the relativity of the term "West," pointing out that to a Pennsylvanian, Cincinnati is in the "West," while to Baptiste, the "West" is the country of the Snake Indians, beyond the Rockies. Catlin's observations are interesting in two senses; first, there was still a "West" to dream of in his day; and, second, even then he saw that this "West" would someday end. The Mandan village represented for Catlin the uniqueness of the American West in the existence of the primitive life.

Catlin took great pains to record accurately this fast-passing state of life. Almost one half of his first volume is devoted to the Mandans. This intriguing tribe merited such treatment for both intrinsic and extrinsic reasons: intrinsically, because the Mandans had developed a complex, successful culture based upon both an agricultural and a hunting economy; extrinsically, because the Mandans were soon to be nearly obliterated by a smallpox epidemic. Catlin wished for "the pen of an Irving or Cooper—the pencil of a Raphael or Hogarth" (*NAI*, I, 80) to do justice to the scenes he witnessed in the Mandan village. Yet our artist-author does well enough with his own talents.

Basically, he uses the Mandans as representatives of Indian life, and by the use of particular examples he depicts the same aspects of Indian life which he had more universally described in his opening chapters. Letter No. 11, from "Mandan Village, Upper Missouri," discusses Mandan housing—earth lodges forty to sixty feet in diameter. These structures housed their inhabitants quite comfortably through the prairie winter and summer. Here the reader is often reminded of Thoreau's symbolic use of the house in *Walden*. Letter No. 12 describes Mandan funeral customs, which include platform burials and a subsequent burial of the skeleton, except for the symbolic placement of the bleached skull in a circle of skulls around a horned buffalo skull. Catlin notes that survivors of the dead person would come and visit with the remains, often bringing peace offerings and holding extended conversations with the departed soul. In Letter No. 23 Catlin pursues the possibility that the Mandans are descended from Prince Madoc's band of Welshmen. For this purpose he uses the Mandan's appearance as his major proof, and he draws support from their bull hide boats, which resemble the Welsh coracle. In his next letter he returns from speculation and depicts Mandan costume. In the next he describes Mandan food. Both of these discussions recall Thoreau's use of the Indian as an example of good sense in these "necessaries" of human life. Discussion of meals leads Catlin to Mandan family life, where he destroys the white stereotype of the Indian squaw as an abused domestic animal. In Letter No. 18, he presents Mandan dancing, which, as with other tribes, is a vital expression of their culture. In No. 19 he depicts their sports and other recreations, particularly hunting. And in No. 20 he describes their modes of warfare, which are those of the Plains Indians generally.

This last subject leads him to a discussion of Mah-To-Toh-Pa, The Four Bears, the War Chief of the tribe. Catlin's description of their meeting is worth quoting in order to recall his classic portrait of the great chief:

> No tragedian ever trod the stage, nor gladiator ever entered the Roman Forum, with more grace and manly dignity than did Mah-to-toh-pa enter the wigwam, where I was in readiness to receive him. He took his

attitude before me, and with the sternness of a Brutus and the stillness of a statue, he stood until the darkness of night broke upon the solitary stillness. (*NAI,* I, 145-146)

Letter No. 22, the longest in the book, consists of a full treatment of the Mandan's O-Kee-Pa, their sacred rite of spring. The ceremonies began when the willow leaves were fully grown on the trees along the river bank. At this precise moment the priests ordered the village to prepare for the arrival of Nu-Mohk-Muck-A-Nah, The First Man, the only man saved from the flood, an Adamic figure, who retold them the story of the creation and warned them of the trials to come. The young men began to prepare also for their rites of initiation, and the rest of the tribe's warriors prepared for the Buffalo Bull Dance. On the fourth day of the dances, the figure of O-Kee-Hee-De, The Evil Spirit, was discerned crossing the horizon toward the village. This figure, painted as black as night and carrying a wooden phallus of enormous proportions, threatened the women and girls of the village. When they eluded his advances he leaped on the buffalo dancers in the manner of a bull in heat. When spent, he was beset by the female population, who broke his staff and wooden phallus and drove him from the village. In *North American Indians,* Catlin coyly presents the ribald details in untranslated Mandan, but in his later *O-Kee-Pa* (1867) he translates these passages. With this defeat of evil purposes, the initiation ceremonies began. The initiates had fasted and prayed during the four days of buffalo dancing. Now they were skewered through the pectoral muscles with wooden splinters and raised from the ground by thongs attached to the skewers. They remained suspended until they fainted, in this fashion placing their lives in the hands of the Great Spirit. After they recovered a feast was held and the ceremonies closed.

On this exciting note Catlin leaves the Mandans, or at least he does in his prose account. Before proceeding down the Missouri, he sums up his experiences among these superior people, stressing the major conflicts between primitive and civilized life. First there are the usual elegiac laments, which are given special poignance here by the actual and imminent destruction of the Mandans by a white disease. Although recent charges that the expansionist Amercian republic attempted the genocide of the Indians may seem exaggerated at first glance, an incident such as the destruction of the Mandans by a trader who knew that smallpox had broken out among his boat crew makes a thoughtful American more aware of the real tragedy of the Western experience.

Catlin had experienced these tragic circumstances firsthand, but he also knew the inherent balance and order of the primitive life. *North American Indians* again sounds a good deal like *Walden* when Catlin compares the cupidity of white civilization with the orderly and pleasant life of the Mandans. Speaking of their games and sports, Catlin comments that

> If the uncultivated condition of their minds curtails the number of their enjoyments; yet they are free from, and independent of, a thousand cares and jealousies, which arise from mercenary motives in the civilized world; and are yet far a-head of us (in my opinion) in the real and uninterrupted enjoyment of their simple natural faculties. (*NAI,* I, 85)

Earlier he had made a similar observation about Indian life in general.

> I would say this much, however, that if the thirst for knowledge has entailed everlasting miseries on mankind from the beginning of the world; if refined and intellectual pains increase in proportion to our intellectual pleasures, I do not see that we gain much advantage over them on that score; and judging from the

full-toned enjoyment which beams from their happy faces, I should give it as my opinion, that their lives were much more happy than ours. . . . (*NAI*, I, 61)

No wonder Catlin was so reluctant to leave the Mandans and to go on to St. Louis.

Letters No. 23 to No. 31 describe this slow progress, including visits to the Minatarees, the Riccarees, and the Dakota Sioux. Catlin uses the description of these tribes to elaborate his presentation of Indian life by detailing certain characteristic occupations such as smoking, steam baths, and music. These down-river tribes are also closer to the advancing frontier, and comparatively they are more corrupted by contact with white civilization. In these ways Catlin again and again laments the inevitable downfall of primitive life in the American West.

His emotional response to this life is well-illustrated by an incident which occurred during his stay among the Minatarees. Catlin was watching the Indians racing their horses outside the village, and he decided to enter the competition. Borrowing a horse, he made substantial wagers, not so much in hope of winning, though he was an able horseman, but in order to give some presents under the cover of the bets. When the race was to begin, Catlin learned that he was expected to ride Indian style —naked on a barebacked stallion. The writer's description of his experience is one of the most revealing passages in the book.

Reader! did you ever imagine that in the middle of a man's life there could be a thought or a feeling so new to him, as to throw him instantly back to infancy; with a new world and a new genius before him—started afresh, to navigate and breathe the elements of naked and untasted liberty, which clothe him in their cool and silken robes that float about him; and wafting their life-inspiring folds to his inmost lungs? If you never have been inspired with such a feeling, and have been in the habit of believing that you have thought of, and imagined a little of every thing, try for a moment, to disrobe your mind and your body, and help me through feelings to which I cannot give utterance. Imagine yourselves as I was, with my trembling little horse underneath me, and the cool atmosphere that was floating about, and ready, more closely and familiarly to embrace me, as it did, at the next moment, when we "were off," and struggling for the goal and the prize. (*NAI,* I, 198)

We see here a revelation of Catlin's psychological fixation with the primitive life in nakedly Freudian terms. Yet an interpretation of the passage can be more psychiatric. Thoreau and Whitman describe such moments also, as does Melville's Ishmael and Hemingway's Nick Adams. Here Catlin has escaped to the Adamic innocence in which man existed before his fall into civilization, the same civilization which he regretfully reenters at the conclusion of this volume.

The first volume of *North American Indians* may stand as representative of Catlin's other volumes. This book is his most typical as well as his best. He repeats the structure which he discovered for this volume, not only in Volume II of *North American Indians,* but in all of his other Indian books as well. The journey motif, which orders a systematic discussion of Indian culture, and an anecdotal narration of personal adventures, persists through *Last Rambles,* published almost thirty years later. *North American Indians,* Volume I, remains his best work because Catlin wrote it with great excitement and freshness when he was at the height of his powers. Of course, the volume also contains the most exciting subject—the Upper Plains Indians at the height of their glory. These quintessential Indians are, for most students of the American West, the symbol of the Native American. Therefore, Catlin's depiction of them, in prose as well as in paint, will always remain the heart of his achievement.

Volume II of *North American Indians* uses the river journey up the Arkansas in 1834 for its organizing structure, and it has as its subject the Southern Plains Indians. Yet, for several reasons, it is not as successful as Volume One. Part of the difficulty can be explained biographically. Catlin was ill with fever during most of his trip, and because his energy was depleted he was not able to capture the Osages, the Comanches, and the Kiowas with the same intensity, either on canvas or on paper. The writer had no earlier letters to draw upon for literary inspiration, and his enthusiasm undoubtedly flagged by Volume II. He also weakened the impact of his book by including a great deal of miscellaneous material from his early trips in 1830 and 1831, as well as from his Upper Mississippi journeys of 1835 and 1836. He really should have limited the volume to his 1834 journey up the Arkansas, a trip which provided the most interesting material. As usual, Catlin was hurrying to meet a deadline when he wrote the volume, and his haste shows in its structural and stylistic flaws.

Eight Years Travels (1848) is really a complementary book to *North American Indians.* Although the basic organizing principle is Catlin's own sea journey to Europe, he soon concentrates on his shepherding of three bands of Indians about Great Britain and France. In this experience he reverses the symbolism of the earlier journeys. Here the primitive comes into civilization, in the manner of many Eighteenth-Century satires, and comments upon the contradictions and inequities of civilized life. Although many of the remarks of his Indian wards are incisive and humorous, the book lacks the impact of *North American Indians* because the primitive is simply swallowed by civilization, and Catlin's satire of civilized life seems tame by comparison with Swift, Dickens, or Thoreau. The book remains interesting only for Catlin's biographer, and it has long been out of print.

Life Among the Indians (1857) repeats much material from the first volumes, adding some new material about the South American journeys. *Life Among the Indians,* subtitled *A Book For Youth,* is weakened by its tone—sometimes coy, sometimes breathless when Catlin addresses his young readers. The retelling of earlier adventures adds nothing to the original accounts, and the descriptions of South America seem rushed and simplistic.

Last Rambles (1867) is filled with excitement. In fact, it has more adventure per page than the earlier books; yet at age 71 Catlin had lost the artistic spark which enlivens *North American Indians.* The illustrations are almost caricatures (Catlin called them cartoons), and the prose is garrulous and rambling. Catlin uses the basic structure of the journey, but as in *North American Indians,* Vol. II, he crams in too much disparate material. Marvin C. Ross has conveniently edited the new materials from these later books in his Oklahoma University Press study.

Catlin's other work of 1867, *O-Kee-Pa: A Religious Ceremony,* amplifies and expands material from *North American Indians,* Volume I, which dealt with the Mandan spring rites. The small volume was occasioned by Henry Rowe Schoolcraft's attacks on Catlin's veracity. Schoolcraft was angered by Catlin's refusal to lend his illustrations without compensation, and the Indian agent spent the rest of his career trying to belittle Catlin's work. Contemporary anthropology has reversed the Nineteenth-Century attitude, and Catlin is now regarded as essentially accurate, while Schoolcraft's work is judged erroneous, if not racist, in its treatment of the Indians. Because Catlin was entering into a scientific conflict, he writes a careful, lucid prose supported by colorful but careful illustrations. The details of the ceremonies, the ferocity of the torture, and the ribald humor of the phallic games are all more fully developed. The book was Catlin's last important work before he died almost a decade later.

Catlin's later work, both in literature and graphics, is not up to the level of his earlier success. The disappointments and tragedies of his middle years help to explain such an artistic decline. At the same time, however, Catlin never lost the fervor of his missionary zeal, and all of his productions are marked by the idealism of the true artist. His symbolic depiction of the American primitive is one of the monuments of Western art and literature in the Nineteenth Century, and it remains so for the Twentieth Century. As America, in its third century as a nation, resurrects those artists who lived on the frontier of the spirit, the nation will also appreciate the important achievement of George Catlin in both literature and the graphic arts.

Selected Bibliography

1. Catlin's Works:

Letters and Notes on the Manners, Customs, and Conditions of the North American Indians. London, 1841. 2 vols. (There are numerous reprints and subsequent editions including French, German, and Swedish translations. The most recent edition was issued by Dover Publications, New York, 1973. Michael Mooney has edited a judicious selection.)

Catlin's North American Indian Portfolio. London, 1844. 25 color plates. (This is his most famous collection of lithographs; it was recently reissued by Swallow Press, Chicago, 1970).

Catlin's Notes of Eight Years Travel and Residence in Europe. London, 1848. 2 vols., printed as one. (There are several editions, none recent.)

A Descriptive Catalogue of Catlin's Indian Collection. London, 1848. (This has recently been reissued by the Gilcrease Institute, Tulsa, Oklahoma, 1973.)

Life Among the Indians. New York, 1857. (This is subtitled, *A Book for Youth.*)

O-Kee-Pa: A Religious Ceremony. London, 1867. (This was republished by Yale University Press in 1967, edited by John C. Ewers.)

Last Rambles Among the Indians of the Rocky Mountains and the Andes. London, 1867. (Marvin C. Ross has edited from this volume and *Life Among the Indians* all narrative materials, see below.)

Though most of the Western materials are included above, Catlin published a good deal more on a variety of subjects in book form, pamphlets, and articles. For a full bibliography see Harold McCracken, *George Catlin and the Old Frontier.*

II. Works About Catlin

Balch, E. S. "The Art of George Catlin." *Proceedings of the American Philosophical Society,* 57 (1918), 144-154.

Baudelaire, Charles. "Review of the Salon of 1845." In *The Mirror of Art*. New York, 1956.

Beetem, Robert N. "George Catlin in France: His Relationship to Delacroix and Baudelaire." *Art Quarterly,* 24 (1961) , 129-145.

De Voto, Bernard. *Beyond the Wide Missouri*. Boston, 1947.

Donaldson, Thomas. "The George Catlin Indian Gallery." *Smithsonian Institution Annual Report, 1886,* 265-939.

Ewers, John C. "The George Catlin Collection in the U.S. National Museum." *Smithsonian Institution Report for 1955,* 483-528.

Haberly, Loyd. *Pursuit of the Horizon: A Life of George Catlin*. New York, 1948.

Hunt, David C. and Paul A. Rossi. *The Art of the West*. New York, 1972.

McCracken, Harold. *George Catlin and the Old Frontier*. New York, 1959.

Mooney, Michael. *North American Indians*. New York, 1975.

Quimby, George I. *Indians of the Western Frontier: Paintings of George Catlin*. Chicago, 1954.

Plate, Robert. *Palette and Tomahawk*. New York, 1962.

Ross, Marvin C., ed. *George Catlin*. Norman, 1959.

Todd, E. W. "Indian Pictures and Two Whitman Poems." *Huntington Library Quarterly,* 19 (1955) , 1-11.

Young, Vernon. "George Catlin's Indian Gallery: The Wilderness in a Locket." *Arts,* 31 (1956) , 20-24.

Wasserman, Emily. "The Artist Explorers." *Art in America,* 60 (1972) , 48-57.